T

fro

at   essex eastern
PSA, AKA
Hastings and
        Eastbourne.
                Nags.

Francis Frith's
EAST SUSSEX

PHOTOGRAPHIC MEMORIES

Francis Frith's
EAST SUSSEX

◆

Helen Livingston

FRITH
BOOK CO

First published in the United Kingdom in 2000 by
Frith Book Company Ltd

Hardback Edition 2000
ISBN 1-85937-130-2

Paperback Edition 2002
ISBN 1-85937-606-1

British Library Cataloguing in Publication Data

Francis Frith's East Sussex
Helen Livingston

Frith Book Company Ltd
Frith's Barn, Teffont,
Salisbury, Wiltshire SP3 5QP
Tel: +44 (0) 1722 716 376
Email: info@francisfrith.co.uk
www.francisfrith.co.uk

Printed and bound in Great Britain

AS WITH ANY HISTORICAL DATABASE THE FRITH ARCHIVE IS CONSTANTLY BEING CORRECTED AND IMPROVED
AND THE PUBLISHERS WOULD WELCOME INFORMATION ON OMISSIONS OR INACCURACIES

Contents

FRANCIS FRITH: *Victorian Pioneer*

FRANCIS FRITH, Victorian founder of the world-famous photographic archive, was a complex and fascinating man. A devout Quaker and a highly successful Victorian businessman, he was both philosophic by nature and pioneering in outlook.

By 1855 Francis Frith had already established a wholesale grocery business in Liverpool, and sold it for the astonishing sum of £200,000, which is the equivalent today of over £15,000,000. Now a multi-millionaire, he was able to indulge his passion for travel. As a child he had pored over travel books written by early explorers, and his fancy and imagination had been stirred by family holidays to the sublime mountain regions of Wales and Scotland. 'What a land of spirit-stirring and enriching scenes and places!' he had written. He was to return to these scenes of grandeur in later years to 'recapture the thousands of vivid and tender memories', but with a different purpose. Now in his thirties, and captivated by the new science of photography, Frith set out on a series of pioneering journeys to the Nile regions that occupied him from 1856 until 1860.

INTRIGUE AND ADVENTURE

He took with him on his travels a specially-designed wicker carriage that acted as both dark-room and sleeping chamber. These far-flung journeys were packed with intrigue and adventure. In his life story, written when he was sixty-three, Frith tells of being held captive by bandits, and of fighting 'an awful midnight battle to the very point of surrender with a deadly pack of hungry, wild dogs'. Sporting flowing Arab costume, Frith arrived at Akaba by camel seventy years before Lawrence, where he encountered 'desert princes and rival sheikhs, blazing with jewel-hilted swords'.

During these extraordinary adventures he was assiduously exploring the desert regions bordering the Nile and patiently recording the antiquities and peoples with his camera. He was the first photographer to venture beyond the sixth cataract. Africa was still the mysterious 'Dark Continent', and Stanley and Livingstone's historic meeting was a decade into the future. The conditions for picture taking confound belief. He laboured for hours in his wicker dark-room in the sweltering heat of the desert, while the volatile chemicals fizzed dangerously in their trays. Often he was forced to work in remote tombs and caves

where conditions were cooler. Back in London he exhibited his photographs and was 'rapturously cheered' by members of the Royal Society. His reputation as a photographer was made overnight. An eminent modern historian has likened their impact on the population of the time to that on our own generation of the first photographs taken on the surface of the moon.

VENTURE OF A LIFE-TIME

Characteristically, Frith quickly spotted the opportunity to create a new business as a specialist publisher of photographs. He lived in an era of immense and sometimes violent change. For the poor in the early part of Victoria's reign work was a drudge and the hours long, and people had precious little free time to enjoy themselves.

Most had no transport other than a cart or gig at their disposal, and had not travelled far beyond the boundaries of their own town or village. However, by the 1870s, the railways had threaded their way across the country, and Bank Holidays and half-day Saturdays had been made obligatory by Act of Parliament. All of a sudden the ordinary working man and his family were able to enjoy days out and see a little more of the world.

With characteristic business acumen, Francis Frith foresaw that these new tourists would enjoy having souvenirs to commemorate their days out. In 1860 he married Mary Ann Rosling and set out with the intention of photographing every city, town and village in Britain. For the next thirty years he travelled the country by train and by pony and trap, producing fine photographs of seaside resorts and beauty spots that were keenly bought by millions of Victorians. These prints were painstakingly pasted into family albums and pored over during the dark nights of winter, rekindling precious memories of summer excursions.

THE RISE OF FRITH & CO

Frith's studio was soon supplying retail shops all over the country. To meet the demand he gathered about him a small team of photographers, and published the work of independent artist-photographers of the calibre of Roger Fenton and Francis Bedford. In order to gain some understanding of the scale of Frith's business one only has to look at the catalogue issued by Frith & Co in 1886: it runs to some 670

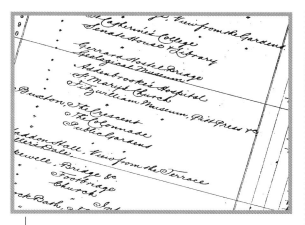

pages, listing not only many thousands of views of the British Isles but also many photographs of most European countries, and China, Japan, the USA and Canada – note the sample page shown above from the hand-written *Frith & Co* ledgers detailing pictures taken. By 1890 Frith had created the greatest specialist photographic publishing company in the world, with over 2,000 outlets – more than the combined number that Boots and WH Smith have today! The picture on the right shows the *Frith & Co* display board at Ingleton in the Yorkshire Dales. Beautifully constructed with mahogany frame and gilt inserts, it could display up to a dozen local scenes.

POSTCARD BONANZA

◆

The ever-popular holiday postcard we know today took many years to develop. In 1870 the Post Office issued the first plain cards, with a pre-printed stamp on one face. In 1894 they allowed other publishers' cards to be sent through the mail with an attached adhesive halfpenny stamp. Demand grew rapidly, and in 1895 a new size of postcard was permitted called the

court card, but there was little room for illustration. In 1899, a year after Frith's death, a new card measuring 5.5 x 3.5 inches became the standard format, but it was not until 1902 that the divided back came into being, with address and message on one face and a full-size illustration on the other. *Frith & Co* were in the vanguard of postcard development, and Frith's sons Eustace and Cyril continued their father's monumental task, expanding the number of views offered to the public and recording more and more places in Britain, as the coasts and countryside were opened up to mass travel.

Francis Frith died in 1898 at his villa in Cannes, his great project still growing. The archive he created continued in business for another seventy years. By 1970 it contained over a third of a million pictures of 7,000 cities, towns and villages. The massive photographic record Frith has left to us stands as a living monument to a special and very remarkable man.

Frith's Archive: *A Unique Legacy*

FRANCIS FRITH'S legacy to us today is of immense significance and value, for the magnificent archive of evocative photographs he created provides a unique record of change in 7,000 cities, towns and villages throughout Britain over a century and more. Frith and his fellow studio photographers revisited locations many times down the years to update their views, compiling for us an enthralling and colourful pageant of British life and character.

We tend to think of Frith's sepia views of Britain as nostalgic, for most of us use them to conjure up memories of places in our own lives with which we have family associations. It often makes us forget that to Francis Frith they were records of daily life as it was actually being lived in the cities, towns and villages of his day. The Victorian age was one of great and often bewildering change for ordinary people, and though the pictures evoke an impression of slower times, life was as busy and hectic as it is today.

We are fortunate that Frith was a photographer of the people, dedicated to recording the minutiae of everyday life. For it is this sheer wealth of visual data, the painstaking chronicle of changes in dress, transport, street layouts, buildings, housing, engineering and landscape that captivates us so much today. His remarkable images offer us a powerful link with the past and with the lives of our ancestors.

TODAY'S TECHNOLOGY

Computers have now made it possible for Frith's many thousands of images to be accessed almost instantly. In the Frith archive today, each photograph is carefully 'digitised' then stored on a CD Rom. Frith archivists can locate a single photograph amongst thousands within seconds. Views can be catalogued and sorted under a variety of categories of place and content to the immediate benefit of researchers. Inexpensive reference prints can be created for them at the touch of a mouse button, and a wide range of books and other printed materials assembled and published for a wider, more general readership - in the next twelve months over a hundred Frith local history titles will be published! The

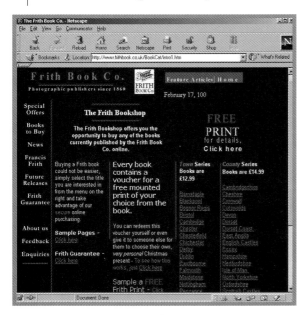

See Frith at www. frithbook.co.uk

day-to-day workings of the archive are very different from how they were in Francis Frith's time: imagine the herculean task of sorting through eleven tons of glass negatives as Frith had to do to locate a particular sequence of pictures! Yet the archive still prides itself on maintaining the same high standards of excellence laid down by Francis Frith, including the painstaking cataloguing and indexing of every view.

It is curious to reflect on how the internet now allows researchers in America and elsewhere greater instant access to the archive than Frith himself ever enjoyed. Many thousands of individual views can be called up on screen within seconds on one of the Frith internet sites, enabling people living continents away to revisit the streets of their ancestral home town, or view places in Britain where they have enjoyed holidays. Many overseas researchers welcome the chance to view special theme selections, such as transport, sports, costume and ancient monuments.

We are certain that Francis Frith would have heartily approved of these modern developments, for he himself was always working at the very limits of Victorian photographic technology.

THE VALUE OF THE ARCHIVE TODAY

Because of the benefits brought by the computer, Frith's images are increasingly studied by social historians, by researchers into genealogy and ancestory, by architects, town planners, and by teachers and schoolchildren involved in local history projects. In addition, the archive offers every one of us a unique opportunity to examine the places where we and our families have lived and worked down the years. Immensely successful in Frith's own era, the archive is now, a century and more on, entering a new phase of popularity.

THE PAST IN TUNE WITH THE FUTURE

Historians consider the Francis Frith Collection to be of prime national importance. It is the only archive of its kind remaining in private ownership and has been valued at a million pounds. However, this figure is now rapidly increasing as digital technology enables more and more people around the world to enjoy its benefits.

Francis Frith's archive is now housed in an historic timber barn in the beautiful village of Teffont in Wiltshire. Its founder would not recognize the archive office as it is today. In place of the many thousands of dusty boxes containing glass plate negatives and an all-pervading odour of photographic chemicals, there are now ranks of computer screens. He would be amazed to watch his images travelling round the world at unimaginable speeds through network and internet lines.

The archive's future is both bright and exciting. Francis Frith, with his unshakeable belief in making photographs available to the greatest number of people, would undoubtedly approve of what is being done today with his lifetime's work. His photographs, depicting our shared past, are now bringing pleasure and enlightenment to millions around the world a century and more after his death.

EAST SUSSEX – *An Introduction*

THE MODERN COUNTY of East Sussex, created in 1974, comprises the eastern half of the old County of Sussex which stretched along the channel coast from the Hampshire boundary in the west to the Kentish hopfields in the east. This severing of the ancient county gave East Sussex the venerable county town of Lewes, perched on its hill, and compensated West Sussex with the ancient cathedral city of Chichester. But strong feelings were aroused, for the old county was the lineal descendant of the Saxon Kingdom of Sussex, founded during the 8th century, and many Sussex people feel that the division should never have been made. None the less, there are distinct differences of character between East Sussex and her sister county. East Sussex has her own identity, visible in these archive photographs and still manifest today.

East Sussex starts just to the west of Brighton and contains most of the seaside resorts that comprise 'good old Sussex by the sea' - Hove, Brighton, Seaford, Eastbourne, Bexhill and Hastings. Among these, Seaford and Hastings have lengthy histories in the defence of the realm as members of the Confederation of Cinque Ports. Here, too, are the 'antient towns' of Rye and Winchelsea, with status equal to the Cinque Ports themselves, but now some way inland: Rye, set picturesquely on its hill, and Winchelsea - New Winchelsea - the shadow of a town that might have been, stranded by the receding sea. The high chalk downlands of East Sussex are far less wooded than the same range further west, truly the 'bold majestic downs, smooth , bare and lonely' of Robert Bridges, and home for many years to the Southdown sheep. The downs culminate in the precipitous drop of Beachy Head, the highest cliff on the south coast. Inland lies the intricate wooded landscape of the clay weald and the heathy heights of Ashdown Forest, home of the former iron industry, which has no equivalent to the west.

In a sense, East Sussex is somewhat insular; although it has been inhabited for several generations by London commuters, which has led to continued gentrification, the county tends to look not northwards towards London, but southwards, towards the sea. The reasons are not hard to find. East Sussex is shielded from the north by the rocky heath and pine-clad heights of Ashdown Forest. Up there you are forced to look south, to gaze on the line of blue hills, the South Downs, which close the view and 'stand along the sea'. Moreover, from Saxon times down to today, Ashdown Forest has been a little wild and untamed. Throughout the Middle Ages it was a royal hunting forest. In earlier days it was the reputedly impenetrable forest of Andredsweald, grazed by swine, and on which generations had to toil with axe and saw to make clearings for habitation - the 'hursts' of the region, such as Ticehurst and Wadhurst. It was a region of iron mines, and was the known haunt of the 'gentlemen', the ruthless cut-throat smugglers, romanticised in more recent years.

Another reason why East Sussex looks outwards, towards the coast, is the sticky, tenacious nature of the Weald clay. This ensured that Sussex roads had an almost legendary reputation for their impassable mire: for a full six months of the year, until the advent of the turnpikes in the 18th century, East Sussex was closed to the outside world. A 'lady of quality' near Lewes had to travel to church in a carriage drawn not by horses but by oxen, and draught oxen were employed on the heavy clay fields. Thus the county could not look northwards overland to London. No, East Sussex looked southwards to the sea, to the channel ports and the river ports on the long estuaries of her rivers, particularly the Ouse and the Rother. Coasting trade and river trade were of huge importance. Virtually every riverside settlement had its wharves, and many were involved in sea fishing and boat-building. Boatbuilding continued in Lewes, for example, until well into the 19th century.

The Channel coast is not tame; even today,

Brighton, The Pier 1889 22345

with big sea defences and sophisticated engineering works, there are fears of coastal flooding. In the past its moods could bring prosperity or wreak destruction. The River Ouse changed its course in the 16th century, leaving the proud, ancient port of Seaford to decline and promoting humble Meeching, the 'Newhaven', to importance. In some cases coastal erosion during big channel storms led to the loss of whole villages, such as Old Winchelsea, or to their partial destruction, as at Hastings and Brighton. Others were left high and dry by the deliberate drainage and development of Romney Marsh and the Pevensey Levels - Pevensey and Rye spring to mind.

East Sussex has a long history, though her prehistory is still associated in many people's minds with the Piltdown hoax. For nearly 50 years this piece of trickery fooled the world that a remarkable Palaeolithic human skull had been unearthed in a sandpit at Piltdown in the centre of the county. Some people have suggested that the famous chalk figure of the Long Man of Wilmington is another elaborate East Sussex hoax, but this now seems unlikely. Certainly the Neolithic causewayed camp at Combe Hill near Jevington is real enough, as is the Iron Age hillfort at Mount Caburn outside Lewes. There are significant Roman remains in East Sussex, principally relating to the iron working industry; there are also several villas, though to date there is nothing so civilised as the West Sussex showstoppers, Bignor Villa and Fishbourne Palace. Undoubtedly the most awe-inspiring Roman remains are the huge walls of the Saxon shore fort of Anderida, known for many a long year now as Pevensey Castle. It was built in late Roman times to keep the marauding Saxons

at bay - which it ultimately failed to do - and later a Norman castle was built within the Roman one. The Roman walls, which have withstood the march of some 17 centuries, tower over the little town of Pevensey, and are pictured here romantically clothed in Victorian ivy.

The stronghold at Anderida fell to the Saxons in AD 490, and all the inhabitants were killed. The Saxons took over the area, and during the next few centuries the kingdom of Sussex came into being. Christianity arrived later in Sussex than in many other parts of Britain, for it was not until AD 681 that St Wilfred came on his evangelising mission from Northumberland to Selsey in West Sussex. Fragments of Saxon handiwork occur in several East Sussex churches: the best known is the 8th-century carved stone preserved in Old Bexhill church.

The most momentous battle and best known date in English history surely must be the Battle of Hastings, 1066, when the Norman Duke William earned his title 'the Conqueror' by defeating the Saxon King Harold II. William landed at Pevensey, which at that time lay on the coast, not about a mile inland as it does today, and marched with his army to meet Harold at a suitable spot on a little hill just inland from Hastings. The town that has grown at the gates of the abbey William founded to mark his victory is known simply as 'Battle'. This alone says more than many words could do for the importance of that battle in the development of the English nation.

The Normans were great church builders, and Battle Abbey, with its high altar at the spot where King Harold fell, was one of their earliest and most magnificent works. The huge gatehouse and several other buildings survive, and are pictured here. Many parish churches in East Sussex were rebuilt from Norman times onward throughout the medieval era.

The Normans were also the builders of proud castles, and under their rule three big castles were built in East Sussex, at Lewes, Pevensey and Hastings. A large part of the last-named castle, which may have stood close to a Roman antecedent, succumbed to coastal erosion in the 13th century. The ruins are pictured here in late Victorian times. Later medieval castles which survive in East Sussex are the famous moated pair: Bodiam, pictured here replete with ivy, which dates from the late 14th century, and the 15th-century brick-built Herstmontceux.

Iron was mined in Ashdown Forest from the later Middle Ages until the 19th century, with many of the deserted Roman mines being worked afresh and new ones opened up. Hammer ponds were created by damming streams to provide a head of water to power the drop-hammers. Furnaces and forges were built, and East Sussex became the 'black country' of Tudor England. It was on Ashdown Forest that the first English cannon were cast; the forges worked day and night to turn out cannon and shot for the navy, while there was a lucrative sideline in railings (those formerly round St Paul's cathedral, for example) and firebacks. The iron industry was no more by the time Frith's photographers took their pictures, but they plied their cameras around several of the villages that had waxed fat during its heyday. These include Wadhurst, Mayfield and Maresfield.

The seabathing craze that overwhelmed genteel England in the 18th century began, in East Sussex at least, if not in the country as a whole, in Brighton - then the half-dilapidated fishing village of Brighthelmstone. A Lewes doctor, Richard Russell, published a treatise on the beneficial effects of drinking and bathing in salt water. It caught the mood of the times; some 30 years later the arrival of the Prince Regent (later George IV) in Brighton secured its pre-eminence among resorts and catapulted the little village to the forefront of 'Fashion'. The prince developed his chief Brighton residence as the mock-oriental Royal Pavilion, and the town began to grow. Hastings and genteel St Leonards, Eastbourne and Bexhill followed suit.

Thus the seaside holiday was born and, as the pictures here show, continued to thrive in the ever-burgeoning East Sussex pleasure-grounds by the sea. So East Sussex passed from being an important industrial area, with little coastal ports and fishing and boat-building villages huddled along its treacherous coast, replete with gangs of desperadoes ready to smuggle in brandy, silk and lace, to being the destination of thousands of holiday-makers.

Equally, since the coming of the railways, the population of East Sussex has risen dramatically, and the demands for new housing grow ever noisier. Villas, bungalows, chalets, blocks of flats, all straining for that all-important view of the sea, mean that today the whole coast is now built up, apart from the National Trust estates between Seaford Head and Beachy Head, including the famed 'Seven Sisters'.

Thus, the settlement pattern visible on today's maps shows that the vast majority of the population live along the coast. The big seaside resorts tend to merge one into another and sprawl inland. Brighton and Hove straggle up the slopes of the confining downs, and Eastbourne has engulfed Polegate. It was not so when many of these pictures were taken. Then, the names still related to individual places. Inland, the pattern of small towns and villages has been somewhat disturbed by growth along the roads, but the fundamental layout has not changed. The centres of towns like breezy hilltop Lewes and pretty Mayfield are very recognisable in pictures over a century old. More change is apparent in the roadside hamlets - but this change is very recent, and is due to the huge press of traffic these roads and lanes now have to carry. These villages, towns and hamlets were self-sufficient. East Sussex was once full of windmills, which crowned many an eminence. Several are pictured here, including Nutley, Rye and Polegate.

There are few 'great houses' in East Sussex. Firle Place, in its superb setting beneath the South Downs, is the largest. But this is compensated for by the charming East Sussex vernacular architecture. Many of the village streets are lined by attractive weather-boarded and tile-hung cottages and brick-built houses. Occasionally sandstone and flint were used where these rocks were available.

The pictures in this book have been arranged so as to present a tour through the county. They start in noisy, bustling seaside Sussex in its Victorian/Edwardian heyday, visit the remnants of the 'ancient towns' of Rye and Winchelsea, and then turn inland across the downs and through the low-lying clay Weald and the county town, Lewes, before climbing up to the wilderness of Ashdown Forest.

Beachy Head, From the Sands 1903 50417

HOVE
The Drive 1898 41895
The trees have grown considerably, obscuring the fine Victorian architecture, and there are traffic lights and other modern paraphernalia, but the Drive looks substantially the same today as it does in this century-old photograph. Note the fine carriage on the right, the Victorian family stepping out and the delivery boy in the centre.

HOVE
Church Road 1898 41896
This bustling view of Church Road with its bicycles and horse-drawn vehicles is dominated by the sadly-lamented old Town Hall, which burned down in 1966. The imposing tower of this fine building held a carillon of twelve bells which played a different tune for each day of the week.

HOVE, THE VICTORIA STATUE 1902 48507

HOVE
The Victoria Statue 1902
Thomas Brock's superb 13ft high bronze statue of Queen Victoria, which stands at the seaward end of Grand Avenue, was unveiled in 1901. It was designed to commemorate the sixtieth anniversary of the Queen's accession, but the Queen died before the statue was completed and the unveiling ceremony was a very subdued affair.

◆

HOVE
The Esplanade 1921
Looking westwards along the Esplanade with the Lawns on the right, the photographer has captured a superb view of genteel Hove, a cut above its altogether more cosmopolitan neighbour, Brighton. On this hot summer's day, three little girls on the bench in the foreground look towards the camera.

HOVE, THE ESPLANADE 1921 71502

HOVE, THE LAWNS 1921 71503
Courtenay Terrace is the only group of houses in Hove with long gardens backing onto the beach. In this view, looking eastwards over the gardens, Hove's famous Lawns are clearly visible, and Brighton's West Pier can be seen. Today, the built-up promenade extends westwards past the houses, but both they and their gardens survive.

HOVE, KINGSWAY ROAD C1955 H128002
Kingsway is Hove's coast road. Little has changed since this picture was taken nearly 50 years ago, save that the traffic is now a constant stream, not the solitary tandem pictured here. The parade of shops still exists and the corner shop is still open, but the Post Office sign has disappeared.

HOVE, BRITTANY ROAD c1955 H128003
Brittany Road runs inland from Kingsway at the corner shop pictured in photograph No H128002. The scene here is not changed greatly today, although there are many more parked cars which line the road and the trees have grown.

HOVE, THE BOATING LAKE c1960 H128006
The Hove boating lake, which is an eastwards continuation of the lagoon on which Shoreham harbour stands, has been beloved by generations of children. In this charming and evocative picture, boys are adjusting their boats whilst parents look on. In the background is Kingsway.

HOVE

St Andrew's Church c1960

St Andrew's is the old parish church of Hove. It dates from Norman times, but became ruinous during the 18th century and was entirely rebuilt in 1836. Today, the church is dwarfed by the town gasometer.

◆

BRIGHTON

The Aquarium 1889

A goat cart awaiting customers is visible on the left of the picture. This is the entrance to Brighton's Aquarium, now the Sealife Centre, which opened in 1872. The ornate clock tower and gateway were added in 1874 to designs by the famous pier designer Eugenius Birch. Both the entrance and the tower were demolished in 1928.

HOVE, ST ANDREW'S CHURCH c1960 H128010

BRIGHTON, THE AQUARIUM 1889 22238

BRIGHTON
The Seafront Hotels 1890 27609
Two of Brighton's famous seafront hotels: on the left,
the red brick Metropole, which opened that year as
the largest hotel outside London, and on the right the
Grand. The Grand was built in 1862-4 in the Italianate
style. It was severely damaged by a terrorist bomb in
1984 but has been restored to its former glory.

BRIGHTON, THE PIER 1889 22345
This 1889 view shows a still undeveloped West Pier. It was built in 1863-66 to designs by Eugenius Birch and was gradually embellished over the years. The West Pier is generally regarded as one of the finest ever built. It is very sad that it has been derelict for nearly 30 years; the West Pier Trust still aims at restoring it.

BRIGHTON, THE WEST PIER 1894 33717
A line of horse-drawn conveyances waits beside the West Pier during the 'fashionable' autumn season, while visitors promenade along the seafront - note the pram containing two infants on the left. The pier is shown replete with its new pier head pavilion and landing stage.

BRIGHTON
The Beach 1898 41890
We are looking east along a lively
Brighton Beach towards the unfinished
Palace Pier at the close of the 19th
century. This picture is full of life,
bursting with boats for excursions,
fishing boats, rows of bathing machines,
holidaymakers, entertainers - one of the
famous pierrots can be seen bottom
right - holidaymakers, onlookers and
numerous stallholders.

BRIGHTON
The West Pier 1902 48495
The twin entrance booths to the West Pier are visible.
Only the one on the right survives. Note the fishing
boats out at sea beyond the left-hand toll-booth.

BRIGHTON, THE FERRY 1902 48508
There was a thriving trade in excursions along the coast and to France. This view shows a ferry, probably the 'Brighton Queen', leaving the West Pier. Well-wishers on the pier wave to the departing paddle steamer.

BRIGHTON, THE OLD STEINE 1902 48522
The Old Steine (pronounced 'steen') is the traditional centre of Brighton - in earlier times it was a broad grassy valley where fishermen dried their nets. It became the town's fashionable centre after the arrival of the Prince Regent. The trams began operation the year before this picture was taken, with the Old Steine as their main terminus.

BRIGHTON, THE DEVIL'S DYKE 1902 48527
To the left of the flagpole can be seen a pier of the Dyke cable car, which stretched across the valley. This vertigo-inducing ride lasted from 1894 to 1907. The places where the piers stood are still visible.

BRIGHTON, NORTH ROAD 1904 B208002
Tramway construction is taking place in the Old Steine. The photographer is looking towards North Road. Note the large number of navvies. The extensive tram network was completed in 1904 and ran until just before World War II.

BRIGHTON, THE CHAIN PIER 1870 B208003
A superb view of the Chain Pier from the west, showing clearly the pier head, which was designed primarily as a landing-stage for cross-channel traffic; it opened in 1823. The pier was soon a fashionable promenade. It was closed amid fears for its safety in 1896 and within two months it was destroyed in a channel storm.

ROTTINGDEAN, THE CHURCH 1889 22255
We are looking across the churchyard to St Margaret's Church. The church, which was renovated in the 19th century, stands on the site of a Saxon predecessor. It was burned down by the French in 1377 along with Rottingdean's inhabitants, who had taken shelter inside it. Even today burn marks are visible.

ROTTINGDEAN, THE VILLAGE 1896 37139
A century has brought no great change to this view of the village, although it does look rather threadbare in this photograph by comparison with today's manicured look. Moreover, there is not a vehicle in sight - quite a contrast to the constant traffic today.

ROTTINGDEAN, THE STREET 1896 37140
The photographer has the undivided attention of a group of children in this quiet wintry view. At the time Rottingdean was home to a remarkable group of people, including Rudyard Kipling and Edward Burne-Jones.

ROTTINGDEAN, THE VILLAGE POND c1955 R62003

ROTTINGDEAN
The Village Pond c1955
A tranquil view of Rottingdean pond, replete with model sailing boats hardly stirring above their reflections on a warm summer's day. The pond was once popular with downland shepherds, but it dried up in 1976, and is now pumped from the well.

◆

ROTTINGDEAN
Tudor Close House c1955
Tudor Close House was a skilful 1920s conversion of much older farm buildings into seven houses. They were converted into an hotel, as seen in this view, but shortly afterwards the building was reconverted back to twenty-nine flats.

ROTTINGDEAN, TUDOR CLOSE HOUSE c1955 R62020

ROTTINGDEAN, THE WINDMILL C1965 R62037
Rottingdean windmill looks rather more decrepit and forlorn today, stranded in the middle of the golf course.
Legend has it that this famous smock mill never ground corn but was used by smugglers for signalling.

ROTTINGDEAN, THE VILLAGE C1965 R62089
We are looking south along the High Street past the Olde Place Hotel, whose brick and flint façade disguises a
16th-century half-timbered building. Rottingdean has a long history; it is named after the valley - 'dene' - which
runs down to the sea. The view has not changed substantially in the past 30 years.

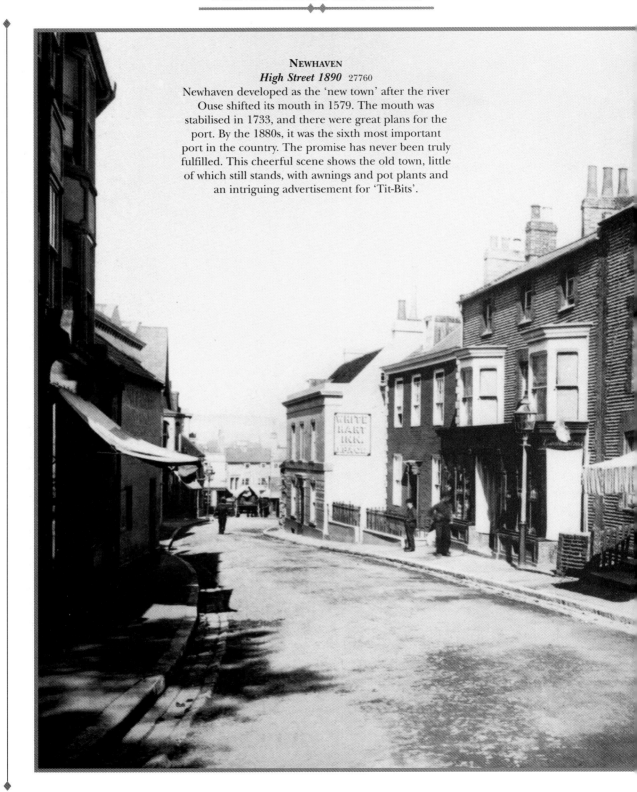

NEWHAVEN
High Street 1890 27760
Newhaven developed as the 'new town' after the river
Ouse shifted its mouth in 1579. The mouth was
stabilised in 1733, and there were great plans for the
port. By the 1880s, it was the sixth most important
port in the country. The promise has never been truly
fulfilled. This cheerful scene shows the old town, little
of which still stands, with awnings and pot plants and
an intriguing advertisement for 'Tit-Bits'.

NEWHAVEN, LEWES ROAD 1890 27762
This is a peaceful scene, with horse and cart on a deserted and remarkably leafy Lewes Road. Today the tranquillity has quite vanished under a complex of industrial and trading estates in the Ouse Valley.

NEWHAVEN, THE HARBOUR c1960 N20054
The cross-channel packet 'Londres' is ready to leave for Dieppe beyond the moored fishing boats. A cargo ship is visible on the left. Newhaven's promise to become 'the Liverpool of the South' has never materialised, and the cross-channel link (transferred here from Shoreham in 1849) has in recent years suffered from threats of closure. Today it is the base for the fast ferry crossing.

SEAFORD, LULLINGTON HILL 1894 34497
We are on the south downs behind Seaford: a now-vanished rural scene, with stooks in the field on the left and horses descending the hill.

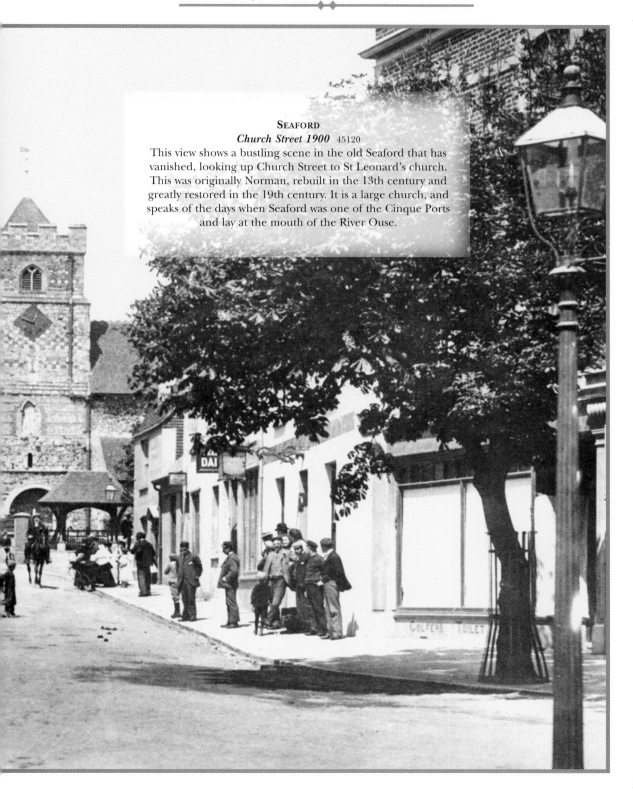

SEAFORD

Church Street 1900 45120

This view shows a bustling scene in the old Seaford that has vanished, looking up Church Street to St Leonard's church. This was originally Norman, rebuilt in the 13th century and greatly restored in the 19th century. It is a large church, and speaks of the days when Seaford was one of the Cinque Ports and lay at the mouth of the River Ouse.

SEAFORD

The Esplanade 1906 55661

Well-dressed ladies, perambulators, hats and parasols
speak of a vanished era in this picture of the
esplanade looking towards the big chalk cliff of
Seaford Head. During Victorian and Edwardian times,
Seaford developed a reputation as a quieter, less
bustling watering-place than Brighton or Eastbourne,
a position it holds to this day.

BEACHY HEAD 1890 25326

This infamous headland, at 536ft the highest cliff on the south coast, marks the point where the South Downs plunge into the English Channel. This picture was taken prior to the building of the present lighthouse at the cliff foot in 1902, when Belle Tout lighthouse of 1831, built high on the cliffs to the west, served to warn shipping of the danger.

BEACHY HEAD, FROM THE SANDS 1903 50417

The red and white lighthouse at the foot of the cliffs is pictured here. It was started in July 1899 and was completed in 1902. The foundations of this 153ft-high tower were sunk 18ft into the chalk, and about 3,600 tons of Cornish granite were used to build it. The light is visible for 16 miles.

EASTBOURNE, THE OLD TOWN 1890 25329
Old Eastbourne - the original settlement - is a mile inland from the coast. This shows a vanished scene, with the unique boulder-faced cottages surrounding the old Star Brewery - the subject of perhaps the bitterest of Eastbourne's conservation battles. This part of the Old Town is now dominated by a supermarket.

EASTBOURNE, THE PARADE 1899 43938
This busy summer scene looks westwards from the pier towards the Wish Tower. Note the rowing boats for hire on the beach with oars propped against the sea walls.

EASTBOURNE
The Pier 1901 48065
Eastbourne's pier, designed by Eugenius Birch, opened in 1872. In 1901 - the year of this picture - two grand salons were built midway along the structure. The theatre at the seaward end was built originally in 1888 and rebuilt in 1899 replete with busy café and offices as well as a famous camera obscura. This was damaged by fire in 1970. The building is now a disco-shopbar.

EASTBOURNE, FROM THE WISH TOWER 1901 48061
This view from the Wish Tower looks east towards the Pier: the water's edge is crowded with bathing machines, while the famous Grand Parade with Eastbourne's finest hotels runs along the left of the picture. The Burlington Hotel, close to the pier, stands on the site of a Roman villa.

EASTBOURNE, THE PIER 1906 56687
Paddling beside the seaside - a picture capturing the gentle care-free mood of a seaside holiday. Eastbourne's famous pier with its pier head theatre complex makes a superb backdrop.

EASTBOURNE, THE LAWNS 1910 62955
Eastbourne's wide and breezy Western Lawns were the place to be seen promenading on a Sunday during the resort's elegant heyday. The land was leased to Eastbourne Council by the Duke of Devonshire. The famous Grand Hotel stands on the right - famed for its Palm Court Orchestra.

EASTBOURNE, THE CARPET GARDENS 1921 71413
Eastbourne's Carpet Gardens are world-famous and of an exceptionally high standard. They were originally laid out over a century ago on the famous three-tiered promenade. The entrance to the pier is on the right.

EASTBOURNE
The Pier 1925 77946
Two charabancs offering tours to Pevensey or the South Downs stand at the pier
entrance - here seen with the three kiosks which replaced the original structures seen in
picture No 48065. They were themselves replaced in the 1940s. The Music Pavilion on
the pier opened in 1924. It is now an amusement hall.

PEVENSEY, THE ROYAL OAK HOTEL 1890 25340

This hostelry, in Pevensey's High Street, is one of the ancient town's historic buildings standing opposite the east gate to Pevensey Castle. It stands across the road from the old Mint House, now an antique shop, seen here when it was three cottages.

PEVENSEY, THE CASTLE 1894 34478

The castle dominates the old town, originally founded by the Romans who built the first castle - one of their chain of forts along the Saxon shore. It was at Pevensey that Duke William landed in 1066 and built his castle among the Roman ruins.

PEVENSEY, FROM THE CASTLE 1902 48225

This view from the castle's east gate shows the same buildings as in picture No 25340. The 14th-century Mint House, on the left, was once the home of Andrew Borde - 'merry Andrew' - a former Carthusian Friar, and court physician to Henry VIII. He advertised his abilities by shouting about the cures he had effected at country fairs, yet he is known to have worn a hair shirt.

PEVENSEY BAY, THE VILLAGE c1965 P50085

There was nothing at Pevensey Bay when Duke William landed there on 28 September 1066, and it remained empty of habitation for many years . Some 300 years ago, a fishing community developed at Wallsend. In the 20th century a thriving seaside resort developed. This view shows shoppers heading towards the stores (note the Hovis sign) on a sunny summer's morning.

LITTLE COMMON, THE WHEATSHEAF INN c1960 L368003

Little Common was an isolated village to the west of Bexhill until the depredations of the 20th century forced its development. The Wheatsheaf is an old-established inn restored in about 1900. It was for many years an important staging post on the Hastings to Brighton turnpike road.

BEXHILL, THE OLD TOWN 1897 38994

We are looking down Church Street in Bexhill's old town, which lies inland from the seaside resort. The walnut tree on the right once marked the old town's centre; it was cut down in 1921. The well-known Bell Hotel is on the left, and in the centre is the partly-weatherboarded Wealden hall-house.

BEXHILL, THE PARADE 1903 50308
This photograph was taken during the heyday of the Cairo and Central promenade; we are looking towards the bandstand and the Kursaal, with a happily-posed seaside goat-cart and donkey. The eastern-style domes were typical of many early buildings of the resort. On the left is the De La Warr Parade.

BEXHILL, THE BEACH 1910 62937
This evocative beach scene shows be-hatted little girls in wind-blown skirts digging the sand, watched by two boys with heavy nets - possibly two fisher-lads?

ST LEONARD'S, THE SUSSEX HOTEL 1890 25366
St Leonard's was laid out by James Burton (father of the more famous Decimus Burton) after 1828. It is still to some extent separate from Hastings, and certainly still that town's genteel 'west end', although the modern town has engulfed Burton's original development.

ST LEONARD'S, FROM THE BOUNDARY 1891 29605
The New Pier (it dated from 1891) runs along the skyline of this view of the seafront, with its former Boundary Archway (separating Burton's town from Hastings) on the right. The people - children and adults - seem surprisingly natural and unposed - a truly happy monument preserved by Frith's photographer.

ST LEONARD'S, THE PIER 1891 29607
The pier was built in 1891 - the year of this picture - opposite the Royal Victoria Hotel and immediately in front of the former Baths, described by a gushing contemporary account as 'such that the most fastidious cannot fail to be gratified'. This pier was severely damaged in World War II and was subsequently demolished.

ST LEONARD'S, THE ROYAL VICTORIA HOTEL 1891 29608
Originally called the St Leonard's Hotel, the Royal Victoria was the first principal building of the new town laid out by James and Decimus Burton. It was opened on 28 October 1829 with a dinner for over 200 people followed by a grand display of fireworks. The name was changed in 1834 after Princess (later Queen) Victoria stayed there with her mother.

HASTINGS
The Beach 1890 25357
This view shows the sea-front and beach, looking
towards the pier. The sands are replete with bathing
machines, boats, children and ladies with parasols:
Victorian seaside gentility. Note the perambulators in
the centre of the picture.

HASTINGS, THE PIER 1890 22780
The pier, designed by Eugenius Birch, opened in 1872. In the following years many buildings were added to it with major reconstruction in the 1930s. In 1891, a year after this picture was taken, a second pier was built opposite the Royal Victoria Hotel, but this was damaged during World War Two, and was subsequently demolished.

HASTINGS, THE CASTLE RUINS 1890 22791
The remains of Hastings Castle, the first built by William the Conqueror, crown Hastings' West Hill, with superb views over the town and out to sea. Coastal erosion, culminating in a great storm in 1287, destroyed much of the castle fabric, seen in this picture as an ivy-covered ruin.

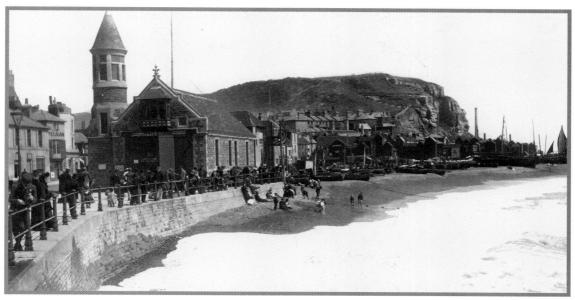

HASTINGS, THE LIFEBOAT HOUSE 1894 34427

The eastern end of Hastings beach beside the RNLI lifeboat house is known as the 'Stade'- Saxon for 'landing place'; here the fleet of about 40 fishing boats are still winched up onto the shingle. On the right of the picture the unique tall weatherboarded net stores cluster beneath East Cliff. The three-storied sheds date from Tudor times, and today are a major attraction.

FAIRLIGHT, THE GLEN 1890 22802

The massive coastal landslides and deep glens between Hastings and Pett have been popular with tourists since the mid 19th century. The coastal landslides occur frequently. In 1980/81 the famous viewpoint 'Lover's Seat' was destroyed.

FAIRLIGHT, THE GLEN 1890 22804

FAIRLIGHT
The Glen 1890
A Victorian party linger beside the 'dripping well' in the deep wooded Fairlight Glen. Here the little stream cascades in a double waterfall over the two bands of hard sandstone rock, and has cut itself a narrow gorge within the wider glen.

◆

PETT LEVEL
The Beach c1955
The stretch of marshland from Winchelsea to Pett is known as Pett Level. This view looks along the shingle beach which fronts the marshland towards Fairlight.

PETT LEVEL, THE BEACH c1955 P258004

PETT LEVEL, BEACH ROAD C1955 P258006
An evocative shot of the mid 20th-century coast, with seaside paraphernalia squeezed between the marshes and the sea. The signs look the part, but the standard of the outside seating has to be seen to be believed.

PETT LEVEL, THE MARKET STORES C1955 P258028
The photographer has moved slightly further back down the road to take in the whole of the Market Stores, no doubt for a picture postcard of the time. Postcards with scenes such as this were popular purchases until relatively recently.

PETT LEVEL, THE VILLAGE c1955 P258011
To the left of the picture is the tall octagonal belfry and spire of St Mary and St Peter's church, built in the 1860s for £2,000. The tile-hung cottages on the right are considerably older.

WINCHELSEA, THE CHURCH 1894 34449
This is a magnificent view of the semi-ruinous church of St Thomas, designed to be a big proud church, but probably never finished. Nothing much has changed since this picture was taken a century ago - an echo of Celia Fiennes writing in 1697 'grass grows now where Winchelsea was, as was once said of Troy'.

WINCHELSEA, THE TOWN 1894 34451
Winchelsea, despite its status, is really little more than a village; it feels like a prosperous garden suburb with its grass verges and widely-spaced houses. Its original population in the 13th century was about 6,000, now there are only a few hundred.

WINCHELSEA, STRAND GATE 1906 53483
This was Winchelsea's north east gate and lay by the banks of the River Brede (hence the name). It dates from the early fourteenth century. Winchelsea was laid out as a "new town" in 1288 on a gridiron pattern with 39 blocks. The town never really grew and today it covers only 12 of the original blocks.

WINCHELSEA, THE TOWN 1906 53491
Winchelsea is an 'ancient' town, like Rye, equal in status to the Cinque Ports and having to provide a quota of ships for the English fleet. A 'new town' was built on the hilltop when the original town was claimed by the sea in 1287. It suffered repeated attacks by the French in the Hundred Years' War.

WINCHELSEA, THE WESLEY TREE 1912 64938
This is the magnificent ash tree under which the ageing John Wesley, founder of Methodism, preached his last sermon on 7 October, 1790. He said of the event 'I stood under a large tree and called most of the inhabitants of the town . . . it seemed as if all that heard were almost persuaded to be Christians'. The tree was struck by lightening in 1927 but another has replaced it.

RYE
Mermaid Street 1888

The old hospital (1576) on the right, so called since it performed that function during the Napoleonic Wars, forms the main subject of this early picture of the most photographed of Rye's cobbled streets, which slopes downhill towards Strand Quay. Its historic buildings, ranging from medieval half-timber to Georgian brick, are well-preserved today.

RYE
Landgate 1890

This still stands on the north-east of the town and is the only one of Rye's four gates to survive. It is part of the fortifications authorised by Edward III in the 14th century. Its portcullis grooves still remain. The clock is a memorial to Prince Albert.

RYE, MERMAID STREET 1888 21161

RYE, LANDGATE 1890 25405

RYE, THE TOWN 1901 47443
Rye, set on its sandstone isle rising from the flat fen of Romney Marsh, still presents something of a medieval picture, dominated by the great church of St Mary. Rye became a member of the Cinque Ports confederation in 1191, at first as a 'limb' of Hastings. In 1336, it was styled an 'Ancient Town'. It suffered much in the raids of the Hundred Years' War.

RYE, THE RIVER ROTHER 1901 47445
The Ypres Tower and the spire of St Mary's church are clearly visible in this picture of Strand Quay and the River Rother. Rye was an important port in the coastal trade, and had extensive shipbuilding yards.

RYE, YPRES CASTLE 1901 47450

Now known as the Ypres Tower (and pronounced 'wipers'), this solemn grey castle was built against the French, probably about 1249, with money left over from Hastings Castle; it is the oldest defence structure in Rye. It was a prison until the 19th century and now houses the Cinque Ports Museum.

RYE, WATCHBELL STREET 1901 47453

This delightful street is named after the watch bell which hung here and was rung to warn inhabitants of approaching French raids. The street was haunted until World War II by the hurrying footsteps of an uneasy little ghost. The steps were never heard again after an Elizabethan house was bombed out and a workman found a string of beads. They were in fact rare black pearls, lost here by one of Elizabeth I's ladies in 1573.

RYE, LION STREET 1903 51078
We are looking up Lion Street towards St Mary's church, the Town Hall and Fletcher's House in summer sunlight nearly a century ago. Fletcher's House, on the top right, is said to be the birthplace in 1576 of the dramatist John Fletcher of Beaumont and Fletcher fame; he also collaborated with Shakespeare on 'Two Noble Kinsmen'.

RYE, THE MILL 1912 64934
The brick and white weatherboarded smock mill still stands in Mill Lane on the banks of the River Tillingham, though it is now converted for use as a guest house. It was built in about 1790, but was almost derelict by the 1930s. It has been restored - but developments have now encroached on the once isolated site.

RYE, ROMNEY MARSHES c1955 R77102

An interesting and unusual view from the church looking across the Ypres Tower to the mouth of the River Rother. The marshes stretch towards Dungeness on the left. Rye once stood on the coast, but from the 15th century onwards silting of the harbour occurred, and Rye is now some two miles inland.

CAMBER, THE VILLAGE c1955 C436003

The sprawling seaside bungalowdom of Camber - the holiday village, camp and caravan site with associated amusement arcades that have grown from the glorious expanse of Camber sands, where the tide goes out for over half a mile, leaving a wide sandy beach backed by dunes.

PEASMARSH, THE POST OFFICE C1955 P257005
The old-fashioned telephone kiosk and the telegraph pole opposite speak of a vanished era. Peasmarsh strings itself out along the main A268 road; its ancient centre of Norman church and Georgian manor house are isolated down a lane to the south.

PEASMARSH, THE HARE AND HOUNDS C1955 P257010
A scene of a typical village pub: quiet, unassuming and somewhat down-at-heel, but an essential part of the fabric of English rural life.

BODIAM
The Castle 1902
The great medieval castle at Bodiam was built in the Rother valley in 1386 against a possible French attack. The massive, romantic pile of grey stone, here replete with ivy, appears to float serenely above its moat.

BODIAM

The Oast House c1965
Oast houses - kilns for drying hops - took on this characteristic 'round house' shape in Victorian times. Today, these Victorian oasts make attractive houses. The hop fields of the Kent/Sussex border have decreased in recent years; modern oast houses are square boxes.

BODIAM, THE CASTLE 1902 48239

BODIAM, THE OAST HOUSE c1965 B128018

BATTLE, THE ABBEY 1910 62967
At the Reformation, Battle Abbey passed to Sir Anthony Browne. The last monk to leave is said to have cursed him with the words 'by fire and water shall thy line perish'. He converted the Abbot's House into his home, which later became a school.

BATTLE, HIGH STREET 1910 62991
It is a sunny day in the pleasant little town in the years leading up to the First World War. The photographer is standing on the Abbey Green - now one vast car park - looking across the market place and up the High Street.

BATTLE

High Street 1921 71507

The motor car is well provided for in this picture, which looks down the High Street to the Abbey gateway. On the right are the Ford Service Depot and Pratt's Petrol. On the left a well publicised garage displays the AA insignia and advertises Shell petrol.

BATTLE
The Abbey Gateway 1927 80411
Here we see a busy day in the Market Place with charabancs and cars parked outside the magnificent Abbey Gateway, which was built in 1338. The little town, named after the Battle of Hastings, grew at the gates of the Abbey built by William the Conqueror to atone for the slaughter and to give thanks for his victory.

CROWHURST
The Yew Tree 1907
Sussex is renowned for her trees: oaks
are commonly termed 'Sussex Weed'.
But it is her gnarled yew trees that claim
the greatest age: this huge churchyard
yew is said to date back at least to the
time of King Harold.

HOLLINGTON
The Church 1890
The village lies inland from Hastings; its
medieval church of St Leonard is
isolated away from the houses among
the trees. The church, with its tile-hung
bell turret, is very typical of the small,
aisleless churches of Sussex. It was dearly
loved by Charles Lamb, who called it 'my
little Protestant Loretto'.

CROWHURST, THE YEW TREE 1907 57235

HOLLINGTON, THE CHURCH 1890 25384

POLEGATE, HIGH STREET C1955   P259025

POLEGATE
High Street c1955

Modernity has overtaken this view of
Polegate High Street, which is more or
less along the line of the 'old (Roman)
road', Farne Street, west of Pevensey.
Polegate grew in importance with the
coming of the railway. Today, the High
Street is choked with traffic and there is
constant talk of a by-pass.

POLEGATE
The Windmill c1955

The large brick-built tower-mill still
stands. It dates from 1817. It was
restored to working order in 1967 -
about 12 years after this picture was
taken - and is open to the public. Today
it stands amid a housing estate.

POLEGATE, THE WINDMILL C1955   P259030

EAST DEAN, THE WAR MEMORIAL 1921 71402

EAST DEAN
The War Memorial 1921
East Dean's simple war memorial fits well on the green of this flint-built village. It is cupped in a hollow of the South Downs, near the famous Seven Sisters sea-cliffs and the onetime smugglers' landing place at Birling Gap. For a long time East Dean itself was a haunt of smugglers and wreckers.

EAST DEAN
The Village Green c1955
A view taken from the war memorial pictured in No 71402, showing the subtle changes wrought in some thirty five years - a flint-built house with brick decoration now stands on the left, creeper has been cleared from the houses on the right and a flagpole has been erected.

EAST DEAN, THE VILLAGE GREEN c1955 E136060

ALFRISTON, HIGH STREET 1921 71422

Alfriston's much-loved High Street and two of its famous hostelries is little changed today. The 15th-century George Inn is on the right, and on the left is the superb timber-framed Star, one of the oldest inns in England. It was originally a hostel attached to Battle Abbey. The alarming lion figurehead still stands outside - it belonged to a Dutch warship wrecked nearby in the 1670s.

ALFRISTON, MARKET SQUARE 1921 71426

A quiet day at the now permanently busy market cross - the only original market cross remaining in East Sussex. On the left is Market Cross House, now the Smugglers Inn. This was once the home of Stanton Collins, leader of the Alfriston gang of smugglers.

ALFRISTON, THE OLD CLERGY HOUSE 1921 71427
This timbered, thatched Wealden house was built in 1350 as a home for local priests. It was the first property acquired by the National Trust, who paid £10 for it in 1896 - and then another £300 to restore it.

THE CUCKMERE VALLEY, THE VALLEY FROM HINDOVER 1921 71428
This view, from the famous High and Over viewpoint on the South Downs, shows the big meanders and flat valley floor of the only undeveloped river-mouth in the south-east. This view looks north-eastwards towards Litlington.

LULLINGTON
The Church 1891
This tiny flint and stone church, capable of housing only some 20 worshippers, is one of the smallest churches in England. It is in fact the surviving chancel of a larger building thrown down in the aftermath of the Civil War.

◆

WEST FIRLE
Firle Place c1960
This is a splendid picture of the magnificent Georgian façade of Firle Place, which disguises the original Tudor structure. Firle, tucked beneath the South Downs and the 718ft-high Firle Beacon, has been the Gage family home for 500 years.

LULLINGTON, THE CHURCH 1891 28396

WEST FIRLE, FIRLE PLACE c1960 F171010

LEWES
Old Houses 1890 22744

This is still recognisably Lewes High Street, with the fine view eastwards to Malling Down. On the right is the Georgian façade of the White Hart, onetime meeting place of the Headstrong Group, who numbered Tom Paine among their members.

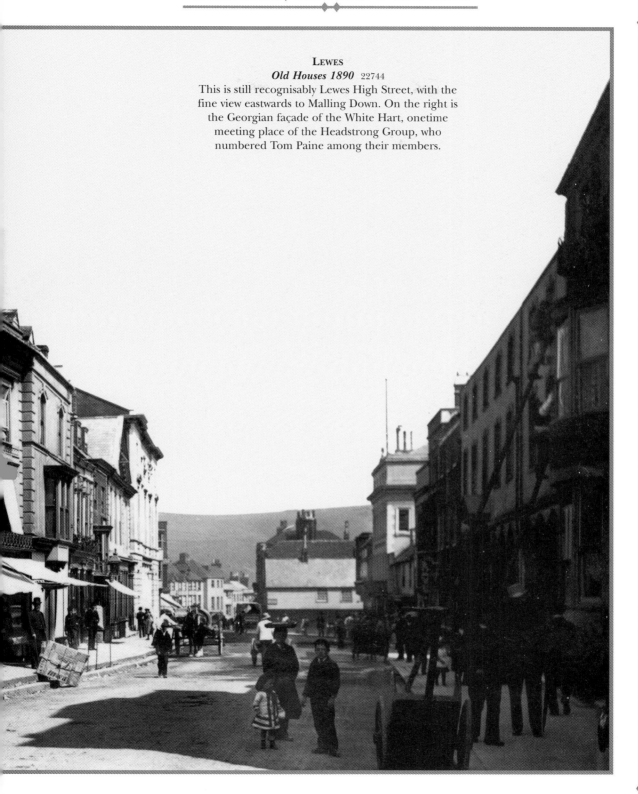

LEWES, HIGH STREET 1898 41906
Hardy Tobacconists are now Caburn secondhand books, while the buildings on the left - now divested of hung tiles - are the secondhand and antiquarian booksellers Bow Windows Bookshop.

LEWES, HIGH STREET 1903 50924
The junction of High Street and School Hill is still recognisable, though the shop on the left-hand corner is now an estate agents and the building is tile-hung. The most obvious change is the replacement of the central lamp standard by the March Brothers' splendid war memorial.

LEWES, SCHOOL HILL 1921 70214
The elegant lamp standard has gone, as have the sun blinds on the house on the left, while Howards House, the building on the right, has lost its top storey and the houses at the foot of the hill have been replaced - but none the less this is clearly School Hill, although the modern traffic system does not allow you to motor down it!

LEWES, CLIFFE HILL STREET 1894 34504

LEWES, THE RIVER c1960 L40080

LEWES
Cliffe Hill Street 1894
Cliffe, across the River Ouse, still has a very separate feel to Lewes up the hill. This view back towards the river from the junction of High Street and South Street has changed little, though the trees outside St Thomas' church have gone. The church was founded in the 12th century.

LEWES
The River c1960
The top of St Thomas' church at Cliffe is visible in the centre of this picture; it was taken from Lewes boating club, which occupies the site of the former Lewes boat-yard and wharves. Lewes was an important boatbuilding centre until after the arrival of the railway.

OFFHAM, THE VILLAGE 1894 34522

We are looking down to the road, the old Lewes turnpike from the slopes of the South Downs at Offham (pronounced 'Oaf-ham') hill; this was the mustering place of De Montfort's unfortunate Londoners before the battle of Lewes in 1264. The scene is hardly changed today.

OFFHAM, THE CHURCH 1894 34524

St Peter's church was built in the 1830s to replace the old church at Hamsey, which was isolated on a former island in the Ouse meadows. St Peter's was designed by Ewan Christian in 13th-century style.

FALMER, THE VILLAGE c1960 F170004
This flint and brick village on the downs north of Brighton is now severed in two by the main A27. The village pond is an old dewpond; it is surrounded by sarsen stones found on the downs. In the early 1970s, it was home to a swan nicknamed 'Fiery Fred' who attacked people.

BARCOMBE, THE CHURCH 1894 34519
An evocative picture of the originally 11th-century church of St Mary and its blossoming churchyard in its lovely isolated setting overlooking the duck pond with good views towards Offham Hill.

NEWICK
High Street c1955

The water pump on the corner of the green is dated 1897 - the year of Queen Victoria's jubilee - when Newick was still a small village. It has grown considerably since then, particularly since World War II. The pump still works.

NEWICK
The Green c1955

We are looking across Newick's green from the pump towards the Bull Inn, famed at one time for the annual sportsman's suppers staged by Thomas Baden-Powell, cousin of the founder of the Scout movement. Most of the buildings round the green date from Victorian and Edwardian times.

NEWICK, HIGH STREET c1955 N90018

NEWICK, THE GREEN c1955 N90026

CHAILEY, THE VILLAGE c1965 C437006

CHAILEY
The Village c1965
On the main A272, Chailey actually consists of three villages, Chailey, North Chailey and South Common. It is famed today for the Chailey Heritage School for handicapped children, founded in 1903, and for its breezy common and restored windmill. In November 1916 the Battle of the Somme was clearly audible from Chailey Common.

◆

ETCHINGHAM
Looking West c1965
This peaceful view looks along the road through this quiet village beside the confluence of the Rivers Dudwell and Rother, renowned for its splendid collegiate church. The Old Etchingham Arms in the centre of the photograph had to be rebuilt in the 1900s after its predecessor burnt down.

ETCHINGHAM, LOOKING WEST c1965 E137023

UCKFIELD, HIGH STREET 1902 48198
This atmospheric view shows a smartly-turned-out carriage driving into Uckfield old town. The view is still clearly recognisable, but there has been much development, particularly on the left, now infilled by a sixties block.

UCKFIELD
High Street 1903 49648
We are looking down the hill towards Uckfield station.
The row of shops on the left has not changed greatly,
but the right-hand side of the picture has now been
developed. Uckfield was a centre of the iron industry
in the 17th and 18th centuries, and was well known
for its brickworks into the 20th century.

FAIRWARP, THE VILLAGE c1955 F136008
The inn's name, the Foresters' Arms, hints that the village stands on the southern hilly fringe of Ashdown Forest. The inn was originally a private house - it was first a licensed premises in 1898. The village is of modern growth. In 1873, there were about twelve houses - and an infants' school was opened 'on the forest'. The name Fairwarp was not used, although the spot was known as 'Fayre Warp' in 1519.

MARESFIELD, THE VILLAGE 1902 48214
This little village on the edge of Ashdown Forest was a centre of the Wealden iron industry. It once had three foundries, the last of which became a gunpowder mill in 1849. It lasted until about 1860, but apart from the old hammer ponds, the old industrial sites have vanished quite away.

BUXTED, THE VILLAGE 1904 52921
Buxted 'new' village - on the main A272 road - was built in the Victorian era close to the railway by Lord Liverpool, who moved the tenants from the old village in Buxted park. Today, the White Hart pub, pictured here, is boarded up and the road is full of busy motorised traffic.

HOREHAM, THE VILLAGE C1960 H329027
This sprawling modern village grew up with the coming of the railway at the junction of the A267 and B2203. It was known as Horeham Road until World War Two, and is now known for the Merrydown cider plant, which was founded in 1946 and is now the dominant presence of the village centre.

MAYFIELD, HIGH STREET c1955   M242032

MAYFIELD, THE VILLAGE SIGN c1955   M242049

MAYFIELD
High Street c1955
Mayfield's attractive High Street, with its raised brick pavements and fine architecture, speaks of the days when Mayfield was an important iron town. It is said that St Dunstan worked as a smith here, and that this is where he had his famed meeting with the devil whom he caught by the nose with his red-hot tongs.

◆

MAYFIELD
The Village Sign c1955
Mayfield's well-known village sign showing a young girl and children in a meadow won second prize (£500) in a national newspaper competition in 1920. Actually, the name probably means not 'Maid's Field' but 'Chamomile field', from the Saxon 'maegthe'.

MAYFIELD
The Windmill, Argos Hill c1955

This fine post mill of 1835 still tops Argos Hill. It has the Sussex tailpost fan-tackle seen on the famous Sussex post mills (eg, Jill windmill, Clayton near Pyecombe). It survived World War I (when demolition was considered, as it was a good landmark for German Zeppelins) and worked until 1927. This picture shows it semi-derelict, but it has since been restored.

◆

FRAMFIELD
Church Approach c1955

The Tudor houses which line the approach to the church of St Thomas a Becket make this corner of Framfield one of the most attractive scenes in East Sussex. The church, originally built in 1288, was one of the first to be dedicated to Becket. It was gutted by fire in 1509 and had to be rebuilt.

MAYFIELD, THE WINDMILL, ARGOS HILL C1955 M242039

FRAMFIELD, CHURCH APPROACH C1955 F139015

STONEGATE, THE VILLAGE 1902 49361
The only traffic is a horse-drawn conveyance in this view of the cross-roads village on a ridge of the High Weald above the River Rother. Today, Stonegate is close to the Bewl Bridge Reservoir.

STONEGATE, THE CHURCH 1907 58581
The church of St Peter was originally built in 1828, but was greatly enlarged in 1904 when the massive north tower and west spire were added. In this picture, taken a few years later, the church still looks new.

TICEHURST, THE VILLAGE 1903 49348
Recognisably Ticehurst: a quiet picture from the early years of the 20th century. The old-established Ticehurst butchers' W J Field is on the left, Coopers Stores is on the right. Coopers took on its present name in 1876.

TICEHURST, THE SQUARE 1903 49349
Ticehurst's attractive village square is all but deserted. The youthful trees on the left are in the centre of the square, where the inn sign for the old-established Duke of York Hotel is just visible.

TICEHURST
The Village and the Church 1903 49352
Children pose for the camera outside St Mary's
church. The church is mostly 14th-century, but was
restored in 1879. Note its short shingled broach spire
and embattled stair turret. It is interesting that the
nicely posed children are all wearing hats.

TICEHURST
The Railway Station 1907 58574
A marvellous view of what was once such an important
part of the English landscape - the rural country
station. This remote station, situated on the Tunbridge
Wells to Hastings line, is actually about three miles
from Ticehurst village; it was at this time known
euphemistically as 'Ticehurst Road'. The station is still
open, but has since been renamed 'Stonegate',
a village which itself is over a mile away.

THREE LEGGED CROSS, THE VILLAGE 1903 49357
An admiring crowd of children - one with a hoop - and some adults linger at this cross-roads hamlet in the High Weald near Ticehurst. The name probably relates to a signpost with three arms - it was recorded as 'Threelegged Crosse' in 1556.

SHOVER'S GREEN, THE VILLAGE 1903 49360
An evocative picture of the signpost and a cart at this scattered hamlet in the wooded hilly Weald south-east of Wadhurst. The name probably means 'the shelving ban" and is recorded as 'la Shalvere' in 1402.

WADHURST, HIGH STREET 1903 49366
We are looking down the Upper High Street, which did not receive its tarmac surface till between the wars. The High Street is renowned for its tile-hung and weatherboarded cottages. It was once an important centre of the Wealden iron industry.

PELL GREEN, THE VILLAGE 1903 49380
The typical white-weatherboarded and tile-roofed cottages of the region characterise this ridge-top hamlet north-east of Wadhurst. This delightful picture shows the road deserted save for a single pedestrian.

COULSEY WOOD, THE VILLAGE 1899 49381
An evocative picture of this attractive village some two miles north east of Wadhurst and now close to Bewl Bridge Reservoir. Weatherboarding - as seen on the inn - and tile-hanging are typical of this area of Sussex. W J Ballard's forge is in the centre of the picture.

BAYHAM, THE ABBEY c1870 5408
The lovely ruins of the early 13th-century abbey - in the tranquil valley of the river Teiser on the Kent/Sussex border - are shown in this picture in their Victorian ivy-clad state. It is the most impressive monastic ruin in Sussex.

CROWBOROUGH, HIGH STREET 1900 44935
Crowborough's rapid development from the mid Victorian era started from the arrival of the railways and the rise
of the commuter. The town - the highest in Sussex - stands at the eastern edge of Ashdown Forest. By the early
1900s it was billed as 'Sussex's answer to Scotland'!

HARTFIELD
The Village 1906 56692
A knife grinder is seen at work in this
atmospheric picture of a deserted
Hartfield. It is a delightful village on the
northern edge of Ashdown Forest above
the river Medway.

HARTFIELD, HIGH STREET 1906 56693
This view looks along pretty Hartfield High Street with its tile-hung and half-timbered cottages. Today Hartfield is best known for its association with Winnie-the-Pooh, whose creator, A A Milne, lived for many years at nearby Cotchford Farm.

FOREST ROW, THE VILLAGE 1902 48265
An evocative view of wide shaggy grass verges, children and deserted roads characterises this view of Forest Row, the Ashdown Forest village that grew up on the site of Royal hunting lodges. The building in the centre is the village hall.

FOREST ROW, THE SWAN 1907 57957

The Swan, which dates back to the Middle Ages, was originally known as the Yew Tree (after a nearby yew) but changed its name in the 18th century when it was a busy inn on the London-Brighton turnpike via Tunbridge Wells.

FOREST ROW, THE VILLAGE 1925 77157

Changes wrought by a quarter of a century are plain to see by contrasting this picture with No 48265. The shingled spire of Holy Trinity Church still rises proudly on the left, but the war memorial and the motorised traffic are reminders that the modern era has come to stay.

FOREST ROW, THE VILLAGE 1931 83750

Here we see a busy scene in Forest Row's attractive centre on the London to Eastbourne Road (A22). Forest Row grew after the arrival of the railway in 1866, and became a parish in 1894. The Royal Ashdown Golf Course opened here in 1888.

BRAMBLETYE, THE CASTLE 1906 56690

This ruinous Jacobean manor house, about half a mile north-west of Forest Row, was built in 1631 for Sir Henry Crompton, MP for East Grinstead. It was sold to Sir James Richards, who fled to Spain in 1683 to escape a charge of high treason. The house, uninhabited since then, has fallen into decay.

CHELWOOD GATE
Ashdown Forest, Beaconsfield Road 1928
80736A
Chelwood Gate stands at the site of one
of the old 'gates' into the medieval royal
hunting forest of Ashdown. This
between-the-wars view along
Beaconsfield Road shows the straight
forest road and one lone delivery boy.
Soldiers of the Portuguese army were
stationed here in World War I.

Index

Frith Book Co Titles

Frith Book Company publish over a 100 new titles each year. For latest catalogue please contact Frith Book Co.

Town Books 96pp, 100 photos. County and Themed Books 128pp, 150 photos
(unless specified) All titles hardback laminated case and jacket
except those indicated pb (paperback)

Around Barnstaple	1-85937-084-5	£12.99
Around Blackpool	1-85937-049-7	£12.99
Around Bognor Regis	1-85937-055-1	£12.99
Around Bristol	1-85937-050-0	£12.99
Around Cambridge	1-85937-092-6	£12.99
Cheshire	1-85937-045-4	£14.99
Around Chester	1-85937-090-X	£12.99
Around Chesterfield	1-85937-071-3	£12.99
Around Chichester	1-85937-089-6	£12.99
Cornwall	1-85937-054-3	£14.99
Cotswolds	1-85937-099-3	£14.99
Around Derby	1-85937-046-2	£12.99
Devon	1-85937-052-7	£14.99
Dorset	1-85937-075-6	£14.99
Dorset Coast	1-85937-062-4	£14.99
Around Dublin	1-85937-058-6	£12.99
East Anglia	1-85937-059-4	£14.99
Around Eastbourne	1-85937-061-6	£12.99
English Castles	1-85937-078-0	£14.99
Around Falmouth	1-85937-066-7	£12.99
Hampshire	1-85937-064-0	£14.99
Isle of Man	1-85937-065-9	£14.99
Around Maidstone	1-85937-056-X	£12.99
North Yorkshire	1-85937-048-9	£14.99
Around Nottingham	1-85937-060-8	£12.99
Around Penzance	1-85937-069-1	£12.99
Around Reading	1-85937-087-X	£12.99
Around St Ives	1-85937-068-3	£12.99
Around Salisbury	1-85937-091-8	£12.99
Around Scarborough	1-85937-104-3	£12.99
Scottish Castles	1-85937-077-2	£14.99
Around Sevenoaks and Tonbridge	1-85937-057-8	£12.99

Sheffield and S Yorkshire	1-85937-070-5	£14.99
Shropshire	1-85937-083-7	£14.99
Staffordshire	1-85937-047-0 (96pp)	£12.99
Suffolk	1-85937-074-8	£14.99
Surrey	1-85937-081-0	£14.99
Around Torbay	1-85937-063-2	£12.99
Wiltshire	1-85937-053-5	£14.99
Around Bakewell	1-85937-113-2	£12.99
Around Bournemouth	1-85937-067-5	£12.99
Cambridgeshire	1-85937-086-1	£14.99
Essex	1-85937-082-9	£14.99
Around Great Yarmouth	1-85937-085-3	£12.99
Hertfordshire	1-85937-079-9	£14.99
Isle of Wight	1-85937-114-0	£14.99
Around Lincoln	1-85937-111-6	£12.99
Oxfordshire	1-85937-076-4	£14.99
Around Shrewsbury	1-85937-110-8	£12.99
South Devon Coast	1-85937-107-8	£14.99
Around Stratford upon Avon	1-85937-098-5	£12.99
West Midlands	1-85937-109-4	£14.99

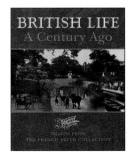

British Life A Century Ago
246 x 189mm
144pp, hardback.
Black and white
Lavishly illustrated with photos
from the turn of the century,
and with extensive commentary.
It offers a unique insight into
the social history and heritage
of bygone Britain.

1-85937-103-5 £17.99

Available from your local bookshop or from the publisher

Frith Book Co Titles Available in 2000

Around Bath	1-85937-097-7	£12.99	Mar
Cumbria	1-85937-101-9	£14.99	Mar
Down the Thames	1-85937-121-3	£14.99	Mar
Around Exeter	1-85937-126-4	£12.99	Mar
Greater Manchester	1-85937-108-6	£14.99	Mar
Around Harrogate	1-85937-112-4	£12.99	Mar
Around Leicester	1-85937-073-x	£12.99	Mar
Around Liverpool	1-85937-051-9	£12.99	Mar
Northumberland and Tyne & Wear			
	1-85937-072-1	£14.99	Mar
Around Oxford	1-85937-096-9	£12.99	Mar
Around Plymouth	1-85937-119-1	£12.99	Mar
Around Southport	1-85937-106-x	£12.99	Mar
Welsh Castles	1-85937-120-5	£14.99	Mar
Canals and Waterways	1-85937-129-9	£17.99	Apr
Around Guildford	1-85937-117-5	£12.99	Apr
Around Horsham	1-85937-127-2	£12.99	Apr
Around Ipswich	1-85937-133-7	£12.99	Apr
Ireland (pb)	1-85937-181-7	£9.99	Apr
London (pb)	1-85937-183-3	£9.99	Apr
New Forest	1-85937-128-0	£14.99	Apr
Around Newark	1-85937-105-1	£12.99	Apr
Around Newquay	1-85937-140-x	£12.99	Apr
Scotland (pb)	1-85937-182-5	£9.99	Apr
Around Southampton	1-85937-088-8	£12.99	Apr
Sussex (pb)	1-85937-184-1	£9.99	Apr
Around Winchester	1-85937-139-6	£12.99	Apr
Around Belfast	1-85937-094-2	£12.99	May
Colchester (pb)	1-85937-188-4	£8.99	May
Exmoor	1-85937-132-9	£14.99	May
Leicestershire (pb)	1-85937-185-x	£9.99	May
Lincolnshire	1-85937-135-3	£14.99	May
North Devon Coast	1-85937-146-9	£14.99	May
Nottinghamshire (pb)	1-85937-187-6	£9.99	May
Peak District	1-85937-100-0	£14.99	May
Around Truro	1-85937-147-7	£12.99	May
Yorkshire (pb)	1-85937-186-8	£9.99	May
Berkshire (pb)	1-85937-191-4	£9.99	Jun
Brighton (pb)	1-85937-192-2	£8.99	Jun
County Durham	1-85937-123-x	£14.99	Jun
Dartmoor	1-85937-145-0	£14.99	Jun
Down the Severn	1-85937-118-3	£14.99	Jun
East London	1-85937-080-2	£14.99	Jun
East Sussex	1-85937-130-2	£14.99	Jun
Glasgow (pb)	1-85937-190-6	£8.99	Jun
Kent (pb)	1-85937-189-2	£9.99	Jun
Kent Living Memories	1-85937-125-6	£14.99	Jun
Redhill to Reigate	1-85937-137-x	£12.99	Jun
Stone Circles & Ancient Monuments			
	1-85937-143-4	£17.99	Jun
Victorian & Edwardian Kent			
	1-85937-149-3	£14.99	Jun
Victorian & Edwardian Maritime Album			
	1-85937-144-2	£17.99	Jun
Victorian & Edwardian Yorkshire			
	1-85937-154-x	£14.99	Jun
West Sussex	1-85937-148-5	£14.99	Jun
Churches of Berkshire	1-85937-170-1	£17.99	Jul
Churches of Dorset	1-85937-172-8	£17.99	Jul
Derbyshire (pb)	1-85937-196-5	£9.99	Jul
Edinburgh (pb)	1-85937-193-0	£8.99	Jul
Folkstone	1-85937-124-8	£12.99	Jul
Gloucestershire	1-85937-102-7	£14.99	Jul
Herefordshire	1-85937-174-4	£14.99	Jul
North London	1-85937-206-6	£14.99	Jul
Norwich (pb)	1-85937-194-9	£8.99	Jul
Ports and Harbours	1-85937-208-2	£17.99	Jul
Somerset and Avon	1-85937-153-1	£14.99	Jul
South Devon Living Memories			
	1-85937-168-x	£14.99	Jul
Warwickshire (pb)	1-85937-203-1	£9.99	Jul
Worcestershire	1-85937-152-3	£14.99	Jul
Yorkshire Living Memories			
	1-85937-166-3	£14.99	Jul

FRITH PRODUCTS & SERVICES

Francis Frith would doubtless be pleased to know that the pioneering publishing venture he started in 1860 still continues today. More than a hundred and thirty years later, The Francis Frith Collection continues in the same innovative tradition and is now one of the foremost publishers of vintage photographs in the world. Some of the current activities include:

Interior Decoration

Today Frith's photographs can be seen framed and as giant wall murals in thousands of pubs, restaurants, hotels, banks, retail stores and other public buildings throughout the country. In every case they enhance the unique local atmosphere of the places they depict and provide reminders of gentler days in an increasingly busy and frenetic world.

Product Promotions

Frith products have been used by many major companies to promote the sales of their own products or to reinforce their own history and heritage. Brands include Hovis bread, Courage beers, Scots Porage Oats, Colman's mustard, Cadbury's foods, Mellow Birds coffee, Dunhill pipe tobacco, Guinness, and Bulmer's Cider.

Genealogy and Family History

As the interest in family history and roots grows world-wide, more and more people are turning to Frith's photographs of Great Britain for images of the towns, villages and streets where their ancestors lived; and, of course, photographs of the churches and chapels where their ancestors were christened, married and buried are an essential part of every genealogy tree and family album.

A series of easy-to-use CD Roms is planned for publication, and an increasing number of Frith photographs will be able to be viewed on specialist genealogy sites. A growing range of Frith books will be available on CD.

Frith Products

All Frith photographs are available Framed or just as Mounted Prints, and can be ordered from the address below. From time to time other products - Address Books, Calendars, Table Mats, etc - are available.

The Internet

Already thousands of Frith photographs can be viewed and purchased on the internet. By the end of the year 2000 some 60,000 Frith photographs will be available on the internet. The number of sites is constantly expanding, each focussing on different products and services from the Collection.

Some of the sites are listed below.
www.townpages.co.uk
www.icollector.com
www.barclaysquare.co.uk
www.cornwall-online.co.uk

For more detailed information on Frith companies and products, look at these sites:
www.francisfrith.co.uk
www.frithbook.co.uk
www.francisfrith.com

See the complete list of Frith Books at:

www.frithbook.co.uk

This web site is regularly updated with the latest list of publications from the Frith Book Company Ltd. If you wish to buy books relating to another part of the country that your local bookshop does not stock, you may purchase on-line.

For further information, trade, or author enquiries please contact us at the address below:
The Francis Frith Collection, Frith's Barn, Teffont, Salisbury, Wiltshire, England SP3 5QP.
Tel: +44 (0)1722 716 376 Fax: +44 (0)1722 716 881 Email: uksales@francisfrith.com

To receive your FREE Mounted Print

Mounted Print
Overall size 14 x 11 inches

Cut out this Voucher and return it with your remittance for £1.50 to cover postage and handling. Choose any photograph included in this book. Your SEPIA print will be A4 in size, and mounted in a cream mount with burgundy rule lines, overall size 14 x 11 inches.

Order additional Mounted Prints at HALF PRICE (only £7.49 each*)

If there are further pictures you would like to order, possibly as gifts for friends and family, acquire them at half price (no additional postage and handling required).

Have your Mounted Prints framed*

For an additional £14.95 per print you can have your chosen Mounted Print framed in an elegant polished wood and gilt moulding, overall size 16 x 13 inches (no additional postage and handling required).

---

* IMPORTANT!
These special prices are only available if ordered using the original voucher on this page (no copies permitted) and at the same time as your free Mounted Print, for delivery to the same address

---

Frith Collectors' Guild

From time to time we publish a magazine of news and stories about Frith photographs and further special offers of Frith products. If you would like 12 months FREE membership, please return this form.

Send completed forms to:
The Francis Frith Collection, Frith's Barn, Teffont, Salisbury, Wiltshire SP3 5QP

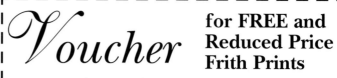

Voucher for FREE and Reduced Price Frith Prints

Picture no.	Page number	Qty	Mounted @ £7.49	Framed + £14.95	Total Cost
		1	Free of charge*	£	£
			£7.49	£	£
			£7.49	£	£
			£7.49	£	£
			£7.49	£	£
			£7.49	£	£

Please allow 28 days for delivery   * Post & handling   £1.50

Book Title . . . .   **Total Order Cost**   **£**

Please do not photocopy this voucher. Only the original is valid, so please cut it out and return it to us.

I enclose a cheque / postal order for £ . . . . made payable to 'The Francis Frith Collection' OR please debit my Mastercard / Visa / Switch / Amex card

Number . . . .

Expires . . . .   Signature . . . .

Name Mr/Mrs/Ms . . . .

Address . . . .

. . . . Postcode . . . .

Daytime Tel No . . . .   Valid to 31/12/01

The Francis Frith Collectors' Guild

Please enrol me as a member for 12 months free of charge.

Name Mr/Mrs/Ms . . . .

Address . . . .

. . . . Postcode . . . .